Lauren,

May God bless
you. Thank you
for your support!

Grace + Peace,

D. Van Ak

5/29/21

# I've Been a Fool,
# *Now What?*

*How to Step into the Future God Has for You*

## Dr. Wendy VanHosen

WESTBOW
PRESS®
A DIVISION OF THOMAS NELSON
& ZONDERVAN

WestBow Press books may be ordered through booksellers or by contacting:

WestBow Press
A Division of Thomas Nelson & Zondervan
1663 Liberty Drive
Bloomington, IN 47403
www.westbowpress.com
844-714-3454

ISBN: 978-1-6642-1261-9 (sc)
ISBN: 978-1-6642-1263-3 (hc)
ISBN: 978-1-6642-1262-6 (e)

Library of Congress Control Number: 2020922509

Print information available on the last page.

WestBow Press rev. date: 12/09/2020

This book is dedicated to the trailblazers of my family whose shoulders I stand upon. To my parents, Willie and Margaret Gray, Grandmother Inez H. Clary, and Uncle Charles F. Harris, Sr. who reside in their heavenly homes, thank you for showing me that greatness is attainable. To my uncle, Salone Clary, thank you for showing me what a genius mind looks like. To my big brother Wendell Gray, thank you for your unwavering support and love. And with very special appreciation to my husband Harry VanHosen Jr., who has shown me a love that could only flow from the spirit of God. Finally, I dedicate this book to my sons Lawrence, Lance, and Lawson, stepson Michael, and stepdaughter Jasmine so that you will know that what seems impossible to man is indeed possible with God.

*At one time we too were foolish, disobedient, deceived and enslaved by all kinds of passions and pleasures. We lived in malice and envy, being hated and hating one another. But when the kindness and love of God our Savior appeared, he saved us, not because of righteous things we had done, but because of his mercy. He saved us through the washing of rebirth and renewal by the Holy Spirit, whom he poured out on us generously through Jesus Christ our Savior, so that, having been justified by his grace, we might become heirs having the hope of eternal life. This is a trustworthy saying. And I want you to stress these things, so that those who have trusted in God may be careful to devote themselves to doing what is good. These things are excellent and profitable for everyone. ~ Titus 3:3–8 (NIV)*

# Contents

Introduction................................................................... xi

**Part 1: Revelation, Reflection, and Reverence**

1. The Power of Understanding Your Identity in God........ 1
2. Religion *Alone* Is Not Enough.................................... 15
3. It's Not Just You ...................................................... 29

**Part 2: Renewal, Reshaping, and Rebranding**

4. Replacing Old Thoughts............................................. 41
5. Perfection Is Not The Requirement, So What Is? ........ 53
6. The Truth About Trouble: It Is Necessary .................. 67
7. Challenging Your Status Quo and Living as an Heir.... 81

Epilogue .................................................................... 91
Notes.......................................................................... 95

# Introduction

As a child, my big brother Wendell and I spent quite a bit of time at our Grandma Clary's house in Portsmouth, VA. Our grandmother played an influential role in our development and foundational perceptions of what was attainable in life. Every Sunday after church, our mother who was affectionately known as "Sister" would take us to our grandmother's house for Sunday dinner. As we sat around the kitchen table, the conversations would always lend to discussions about church service, music, and people within the community. Particular interest was always given to the music, being that my grandmother, mother, and uncle were all musicians. This was also the time when we would hear stories about the hardships of earlier times when opportunities for African-Americans were not as plentiful and about the sacrifices that were made by those family members who had passed on before I was born. It was also during these conversations over dinner at Grandma Clary's house that the idea that I could achieve great things, no matter the obstacles, was established. I would not realize until many years later just how important this exposure to the ideas of beating the odds and excellence beyond adversity, would become.

I was fortunate enough to experience how greatness was made visible by seeing family members get to the other side of struggle through perseverance and faith. It still amazes me when I think about the miles that my grandmother and uncles would walk to and from school. As an educator, I am profoundly moved by this level of commitment towards learning and I've come to understand why my grandmother viewed education as an emancipator over life's circumstances and held higher education in such esteemed regard. This taught me that there is a certain level of appreciation that comes with gaining that which is not easily attainable. Unable to go to college immediately after high school, my grandmother was afforded an opportunity to become a college student with her son and daughter (my mother) at Norfolk State University. Together, they remained steadfast and completed their degrees in music. I can only imagine the unique experience of a mother, son, and daughter being in college together at the same time!

The inspiration for this book also reaches back to the influence of my Uncle Charles, who, before becoming the founder of Armistad Press book publishing company (now held by Harper Collins), delivered newspapers door to door throughout the Mt. Herman community to help the family make ends meet. My Uncle Charles was a visionary in his own right who developed a business acumen from the humble beginnings of delivering newspapers and collecting coins from those he delivered to. I didn't realize it at the time but my witness to these conversations and experiences were establishing and shaping my perspectives not only on great possibilities but on religion and God.

The conversations around the kitchen table at my grandmother's house would become especially lively when my Uncle Charles, Uncle Salone, Uncle Lump, Uncle Ambrose, and Uncle Roland would come together. While cracking open steamed crabs over newspapers spread out across the table, conversations were jovial, loud, and somehow empowering all at the same time. Even in this atmosphere of reminiscing of challenges and times of lack, one could sense that there was little tolerance for excuses, laziness, and self-pity, but always a push towards something greater. As shared by Vincent Harding in the forward of Howard Thurman's book, *Jesus and the Disinherited*, oppression and injustice do not absolve us from the responsibility to courageously pursue a path of integrity and creativity.[1]

My Grandma Clary valued the principles of perseverance, strength, and fortitude and would often use the word "fool" to describe someone whom she felt was wasting their life away. When my grandmother would use the word fool to describe someone in our community, family (yes, family members were not excluded!), or local ministry, as a child I remember feeling as though the word "fool" was such a harsh critical term that seemed contradictory to the Christian values I was

[1] Howard Thurman, Jesus and the Disinherited, (Boston, Massachusetts: Beacon Press, 1996).

being taught. After all, no one ever used the word "fool" in any of my Vacation Bible School lessons. It wasn't a word that I could remember our pastor using in any sermon. When I would eavesdrop on the grown folks' conversations between my Grandma Clary, my uncles, and my mother and would hear my Grandma Clary say things like, "He is just an old fool!", I would chuckle to myself. But I also wondered "why would she say that about that person?" Is that loving others like God says we are supposed to?". In my childlike thoughts, I would wonder why she would use such an unkind word like "fool". But just as the Apostle Paul writes in 1 Corinthians 13:11 (NIV), When I was a child, I talked like a child, I thought like a child, I reasoned like a child. I did not have the maturity and experiences of life to fully understand and process what was being said. I suppose this is the reason why my older family members would say that children were to stay out of grown folks' conversations.

As I have matured in my faith and experienced many facets of life, I'm now forever so grateful to my grandmother for this reference of the word fool. I have learned that it is not a word of condemnation but one that gives way to correction. Fool means to have a lack of understanding, and if recognized, it is an opportunity for growth. I believe one of the reasons that God has led me to write this book is because there is a gap in literary resources for the believer who identifies with the mistakes of the fool and desires to understand how to live life differently in the "now what?". For me, the recognition of my foolish ways ultimately gave way to me accepting my call to ministry and preaching my initial sermon entitled the namesake of this book "I've Been a Fool, Now What?". I wonder what awaits you in God as you embrace the "now what?" in your life. What revelation will you receive? What is the blessing that you will step into?

According to Online Etymology Dictionary, the word fool evolved from the Vulgar Latin word follis which meant windbag, an empty-headed person."[2] In other words, a fool is one whose thoughts are empty and void of truth and understanding. Yet, if we are honest it is a description that most all of us can relate to at one station of life or another. I would go as far as to say that if there are no instances in your life that you can identify with being a fool, you have not grown into the fullness of what God desires for your life. While it is not God's desire that we function as fools, it is quite often through our foolish mistakes and failures that we are able to increase our faith and understand truth.

It is believed that these words found in the New Testament book of Titus Chapter 3, verses 3–8 were written between the years 63 and 65 AD, nearly two thousand years ago from our current 21st century.[3] Yet these words are as timely and applicable today as they were at the time of the Apostle Paul's penning of this epistle. Paul's intended audience for the message of his letter was not the unbeliever, the unchurched, nor those who were worshipping idol gods. But he fashions this letter first

---

[2] https://www.etymonline.com/search?q=fool

[3] https://www.biblica.com/resources/scholar-notes/niv-study-bible/intro-to-titus/

to Titus who was a pastor and son in the ministry and then to the Christians who were located on the island called Crete. How interesting is it that Paul would take the time to remind a pastor and necessarily his congregation of believers that at one time or another, we too were foolish.

This idea of being foolish is not singular to this passage. In fact, the words fool, fools, foolish, foolishly, and foolishness appear in the Bible a combined total of 199 times, including 76 verses in the book of Proverbs.[4] Not only does God want us to be able to recognize when we are being foolish, we have a plethora of references in the Bible to emphasize the point. It is often said that if something is repeated in the Word of God, it is to emphasize God's point and to ensure that we do not miss the meaning of what is being said. As it pertains to "fools", the number of references in the Bible gives us an idea of how important this idea is to God that we gain an understanding of truth and our identity in God, so that we do not function as life-long fools.

To be a fool is ultimately a lack of understanding of your identity in God. Once you gain an understanding of who you are as a son or daughter of God, you come into a new awareness. In fact, so much so that you become a new creature. Therefore, if anyone is in Christ, the new creation has come; the old has gone, the new is here! (2 Corinthians 5:17, NIV) In this sense, gaining this type of understanding is akin to gaining a liberating education about our identity in God. Renowned educator Paulo

---

[4] The Bible, King James Version

Freire asserts in his book, *Pedagogy of the Oppressed*, that an awakening or *conscientization* precipitates a liberation that is praxis, causing men and women to reflect and take action to transform the world as they themselves are transformed from the inside out.[5] This means that we can expect to experience a continuous personal awakening as we are continuously being spiritually transformed. For this reason, I have divided this book into two sections. Part I - Revelation, Reflection, and Reference which is largely focused on self-reflection and Part II - Renewal, Reshaping, and Rebranding which focuses on action and practical application.

Once you've come into an awakening that you've been living through a mindset that is beneath your identity in God, once you realize "I've Been a Fool", the question that must follow is "Now what?". It is in these moments, that we must decide whether we will run towards God for direction and wisdom or will we continue in our folly attempting to live life on our own terms. It is my prayer that you will use this book as a tool as you reflect and navigate through the "Now what?" moments of your life. Both prayer and praise have been life-giving for my journey and I have included moments of prayer and praise at the end of each chapter. I invite you to journey through this book with me and I trust that God will speak life to you. Let's get started!

---

[5] Pablo Freire, Pedagogy of the Oppressed (New York: Continuum, 2000).

# PART I

*Revelation, Reflection, and Reverence*

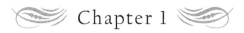 Chapter 1

# The Power of Understanding Your Identity in God

T here is an inextricable connection between understanding our identity in God and being able to limit our instances of foolish mistakes and overcoming them when we do err. Our ability to walk authentically in the fullness of the power and authority that God provides begins with a personal revelation of who we are in God and our decision to accept Jesus into our hearts as Lord and Savior. Until this knowledge becomes personal, it is just simply information for consideration. A personal encounter with God that prompts a personal decision to surrender our lives to God is the door opener to understanding our identity. The closer we draw to God the Creator, the more we understand about ourselves as His creation in His image. In fact, I describe this process as God introducing us to our real selves. The authentic, unique version of yourself that God designed with purpose and potential, not the self that tries to emulate others. We are each a one of a kind, original creation. Even an identical twin has unique differences from the sibling who shared the same space in their mother's womb. An example being that identical twins may look the same, but their fingerprints are not the same, and the imprint or indelible mark that they leave on the world is also not the same. Of course, this is by God's design so that each of us has an opportunity to leave our unique stamp or fingerprint on all that we touch within this world. While identical twins have the same genetic blueprint, each has a unique life blueprint established by God. The Reverend Dr. Martin Luther King once preached a sermon titled "What Is Your Life's Blueprint?" In this sermon, Dr. King reminded us that we must have such a determination for excellence that we do life "so well that the living, the dead, or the unborn couldn't be you any better" than you.[6] In other words, no one can duplicate who you are. For this reason, we are most effective when we operate as our authentic selves. Yet a common human proclivity is to try to mimic the personality of another individual as a path to attain what is perceived as success. For example, seeking to preach like another preacher, talk like another, dress like another, etc., not realizing that which we see is only a small portion of the full essence of a person. It's been my experience

---

[6] https://projects.seattletimes.com/mlk/words-blueprint.html

that those who walk in great anointing have experienced great struggle and continue to be greatly tested. This is why it is fruitless to try and copy another person's anointing when you have not lived the experiences and struggles that produced the surety and confidence in God that accompanies their anointing. You are more powerful walking in your authentic self in God than you could ever be walking as a counterfeit version of someone else.

Further, I suggest that at the basis of our folly is a lack of understanding. More specifically, it is often a lack of understanding of the proper role of those who speak into our lives. "Understanding is a wellspring of life to him who has it, but the correction of fools is folly" (Proverbs 16:22 NKJV). Certainly I'm not suggesting that we cannot learn from a pastor, mentor, or leader within a particular industry—quite the contrary. I'm suggesting that we are to learn from these individuals but that we must remember that our identity is established by God alone, not based on perceptions of even the most influential people in our lives. There will likely come a time where you will need to grow beyond the perceptual parameters of those closest to you in order to operate in the fullness of who you are. Also, the danger in trying to define ourselves based on what we believe about another person is that people do not have the capacity to meet our every expectation. If we have built our identity on people, our idea of who we are becomes shaky when the people we look to for purpose undoubtedly disappoint or falter. There is only one sure source that establishes our identity and purpose without falter and that is God alone. We do not have to worry about God changing our identity in Him or His purpose for our lives. The Word of God says, "I am the Lord, and there is no other, apart from me there is no God (Isaiah 45:5 NIV)." God is the "I am, that I am," meaning that God was before anything else ever existed (Exodus 3:14 KJV). God is alpha and omega, meaning that God is the only one who knows the completeness of each of us (Revelation 1:8 NIV).

Many people identify themselves based on their occupation, gifts, callings, or role they play in relationships and social structures. These items describe what you do and may indicate a certain title or role that you occupy, but they do not get to the heart or essence of who you are. Who you are does not shift based on an occupation or role. This is why you can change jobs or lose a job and still be significant to God. There are numerous verses in the Bible that inform us of just how valuable we are. I will not attempt to dissect every verse in the Bible that affirms our value but will offer several verses here that I believe to make the point.

**You are here on purpose!**

> So God created mankind in his own image, in the image of God he created them; male and female he created them. (Genesis 1:27 NIV)

For I know the plans I have for you, declares the Lord, plans to prosper you and not to harm you, plans to give you hope and a future. (Jeremiah 29:11 NIV)

**You are loved!**

For God so loved the world that he gave his one and only Son, that whoever believes in him shall not perish but have eternal life. (John 3:16 NIV)

**You were created for good!**

For we are His workmanship, created in Christ Jesus for good works, which God prepared beforehand, that we should walk in them. (Ephesians 2:10 NKJV)

In the same way, let your light shine before others, that they may see your good deeds and glorify your Father in heaven. (Matthew 5:16 NIV)

**You are chosen!**

But you are a chosen people, a royal priesthood, a holy nation, God's special possession, that you may declare the praises of Him who called you out of darkness into His wonderful light. (1 Peter 2:9 NIV)

## You are _more than_ your circumstances!

Yet in all these things we are more than conquerors through Him who loved us. *You are more than a conqueror through Christ Jesus!* (Romans 8:37 NKJV; italics added)

## You are righteous!

This righteousness is given through faith in Jesus Christ to all who believe. There is no difference between Jew and Gentile. (Romans 3:22 NIV)

## You are an heir!

Now if we are children, then we are heirs; Heirs of God and co-heirs with Christ, if indeed we share in his sufferings in order that we may also share in his glory. (Romans 8:17 NIV)

These affirmations of who you are in God are reminders of your value. These declarations are not established by humankind, so they cannot be invalidated by the thoughts, actions, or opinions of people. This is important because so many of us have allowed others to have more power in our lives than God's Word. Please get this revelation! There is *nothing* that someone can say or do to you that will change who you are to God!

I share the following experience with you to help illustrate how understanding our identity connects with our ability to overcome great challenges, foolish ways of thinking, and experience a profound "Now What?" with God. For a period of time during my teenage years, I struggled to figure out how to fit in with my peers and made some rather foolish decisions in doing so. Although we went to church every Sunday, I did not have a personal relationship with God. Despite being in church every Sunday, attending Vacation Bible School every summer, and being baptized at the age of eleven, I did not know or understand who I was to God. I was familiar with the religious experience of regularly attending church, but I lacked a true and personal relationship with God. So I sought validation and value through relationships with my peers. From the outside, it looked as though I was sure of myself and confident, but even at an early age I had learned how to mask my insecurities.

At the age of fifteen, I decided that I wanted to get a job and felt that this would make me feel more mature than I was. So my mother took me to a local office where I completed a job application. A few days afterward, the man who conducted the interview called and stated that he needed me to turn in some additional information and provided me with an address to bring it to. When I arrived, he pinned me down and sexually assaulted me. It would be several years before I articulated these words to anyone. Shame and fear have a way of silencing you.

To an already unstable self-confidence, this trauma only added to my desire for validation of my worth. Instead of seeking God, I began to seek validation from the wrong places, or should I say the wrong people. Brokenness has a tendency to attract brokenness. In hindsight, I realize that my thinking and reasoning were produced from a place of brokenness, but it was also the result of a lack of understanding of my identity in God. As a result, I spent many years going around the same mountain of dysfunctional relationships and made many foolish mistakes in the midst of it all. God will allow us to repeat mistakes when we are unable to see our faulty thinking that contributed to the mistake, just as a fool repeats the folly (Proverbs 26:11, NKJV). My rebellion certainly seemed justified given the trauma I experienced but such rebellion was only a masked indicator of confusion and pain, all hidden behind a focus on external appearance to gain the affirmation of others. More importantly, I've learned that we cannot allow the gravity and validity of our pain to justify wayward foolish behaviors, behaviors that are beneath our identity in God. Living life based on the parameters of what someone else did to you will result in you being stuck and immobilized, living below God's desire for your life. It will keep you in cycles of dysfunction because you have unknowingly given power to the person who injured you. When power is given to the person who caused the injury, you subconsciously seek solutions from a source that harmed you instead of seeking solutions from the one source (God) who can not only heal you but make you whole. People do not have the ability to make you whole, only God can.

Through prayer, we can learn to operate in the currency of forgiveness that reaches into the spiritual realm and extends beyond our present suffering and blesses our future. In the spiritual realm, forgiveness separates what they did to you from who you are so that your future is no longer sabotaged by what they did. Jesus taught us about the power of forgiveness from the cross. Jesus took time to ask our Father God to "forgive them" because he recognized the power of forgiveness, releasing their (and our) offense so that He could fulfill God's plan of salvation. We are not able to fully fulfill what God has called us to do if we hold on to their offense. Releasing them, releases you to step into all that God has created you to be. Forgiveness has nothing to do with their decision, but everything to do with yours. Please do not wait for them to figure out who you are before making a decision to forgive. When people do not know who you are, they will mistreat you, mishandle you, and underestimate your divine purpose. The question is not if they will realize who you are, but rather the indispensable truth is that *you* must know who you are. When we finally come into the knowledge and understanding of who we are in God through Christ Jesus, everything changes!

---

*When we finally come into the knowledge and understanding of who we are in God through Christ Jesus, everything changes!*

---

Coming into this revelation of true identity in God will change your response to life's great challenges and your response to tremendous blessings. I call this revelatory response, our "Now What?". No longer did I look to people for validation. No longer do you have to operate from a victim status when victory through Jesus is available to you. The revelation of our identity makes way for an understanding of our worth in God. Once we have a personal revelation of who we are in God, it changes our approach and response to life. Understanding our identity also means recognizing that we have a responsibility to live our best life yet in God, even in spite of great tragedy and challenge. Most importantly I had to learn that my life isn't about what someone else did. God does not intend for us to live life in bondage to what they did. Yes, it happened. Yes, it was traumatic. Yes, it was wrong. However, it was *my* personal transformation through the Holy Spirit that allowed me to walk in freedom. It was not about changing the offender. As my pastor, Dr. Melvin O. Marriner has often said, "Blaming them does not help me to move forward." Forgiving them is a much better course of action because it releases you from being in bondage to injury. That's not a popular message for those who have been victimized and oppressed, because our focus is generally on the offender. But, God requires us to take part in our deliverance and participate in our freedom. Our part is to make a decision to be in a personal relationship with God and to intentionally and continually seek God's will, being willing to surrender our heart, soul, and mind. If not, you may find that you've attained external markers of liberation and success but remain in internal bondage. We have the responsibility of doing what we can humanly do to reach our fullest potential, and God does the supernatural that we as humans cannot do.

---

*But, God requires us to take part in our deliverance and participate in our freedom.*

---

The processes and insights that I have described in a few paragraphs have taken me decades to reach the crucible of truth. What is now packaged together as a succinct series of events was actually full of an amalgam of ups and downs, highs and lows, setbacks, and even some noted accomplishments. Growth is messy. For so many years, I did not have the capacity to seek healing because I honestly didn't know that something inside was broken. I believed that if I just focused my attention on the areas of my life that seemed well, then I would be fine. See, it is possible to have great internal affliction in one area and experience great success in another area. It's not always all-encompassing. But brokenness has a way of showing up at inconvenient times and it will make itself known through foolish decision making. The enemy is banking on gaining a foot hole in your area of brokenness to accomplish his intentions which are to steal, kill, and destroy you. Satan's motives are consistent while his schemes may vary. The enemy operates on the false premise that if he can disrupt your life enough and fill your mind with enough thoughts of defeat and worthlessness before you realize who you are, he can zap your potential for greatness. If he can get you to think defeated, you will act accordingly. But friends, I have good news for you ... ... THE DEVIL IS A LIAR! You were created for good works!

Understanding your identity corrects your vision, unclouds your lens, affirms your value, and helps to clarify how we are to respond when it seems that we have trouble on every side. However, understanding your identity in God does not prevent you from experiencing trouble. Your understanding allows you to have a response that reflects hope, despite the trouble. The Bible tells us in 1 Peter 4:12–13 (KJV), Beloved, think it not strange concerning the fiery trial which is to try you, as though some strange thing happened unto you. In fact, we can rejoice because of the expectation we can have in God. I will talk more about this in Chapter 6, but for now, know that God is greater than any trouble that you have faced, are currently facing, or will face. Finally, understanding our identity in God allows us to experience seasons of life from a perspective of overflow. I am not speaking of an overflow of any material possession. I believe God desires that we experience an overflow of His love, peace, and joy. The bible says it's out of the overflow of the heart that the mouth speaks. God is concerned with the condition of your heart, spiritually. God desires for your heart to be so full of His Truth that you are able to speak to any circumstance from the overflow that is in you. Get to know the truth about who God says you are and let it take hold in your heart, and let it be an overflow out of your mouth and in your life to the glory of God.

**Questions for your consideration…**

1. Reflect on your personal understanding of your identity in God. What comes to mind?

2. How has your understanding of your identity in God influenced your response to challenges? To blessings?

3. What has God revealed to you about you?

# 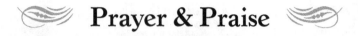 Prayer & Praise

Everlasting Father, I am grateful for who you are and for who you have created me to be. Thank you for the earthly opportunity of time and space to draw near to you and know truth. Oh God, in your infinite wisdom and providence you created me to be your very own with a hope and a future that no one can extinguish. Father, thank you for your transforming power and indelible mark of truth in my life. Help me Lord to see myself as you see me. Help me Lord to walk in the fullness of who you have created me to be. Release me from the chains of blame and shame and help me to walk in the liberty available through Your Spirit. There is no weapon formed against me that will prosper. I am able to accomplish all that I have been created to do through Christ Jesus. So Father I praise you with my spirit and truth. I will not let the rocks cry out when you have given me breath. You've said, let everything that have breath praise the Lord. So in all things and at all times, I give you praise with my mouth, glory and honor through my life. In the name of Jesus. Amen.

# Chapter 2

# Religion *Alone* Is Not Enough

I n this chapter, I propose that we make a distinction between religion, relationship with God through Jesus Christ, and God alone. Our understanding of these distinctions is critical to our ability to walk in the power and authority that is available to each of us through God's Holy Spirit. God desires that we have the courage to turn away from foolish faulty ways of thinking that keep us stuck, bound, and circling the same mountains, but turn towards a path that challenges the status quo, mediocrity, and injustice. I'm speaking of a life that reflects a demonstration of the greatest version of ourselves as a contribution to the world, which by doing so glorifies God.

In my estimate, religion is humankind's attempt to provide a human expression for that which is divine. Many have found difficulty with defining religion because the boundaries between religion and psychology, philosophy, or sociology can be blurred. For example, it is sociologist Emile Durkheim's definition of religion that emphasizes inclusive systems of beliefs and practices that are concerned with worshipping and honoring that which is considered sacred in order to form a shared social structure.[7] Clearly the distinctiveness of religious beliefs and practices may look very different across Christian denominations and other faith traditions throughout the world. If we just consider the practice of baptism in Christian denominations, we can note that for the Baptist baptism must include complete submersion but for the Lutheran, Methodist, and Presbyterian sprinkling or pouring water on the head is appropriate, and for the Quakers and the Unitarian, baptism is not practiced at all.[8] These differences of practice within Christian denominations are largely due to variances in doctrine. By the same token, those who adhere to non-Christian faith traditions such as Muslims share a common belief with Christians in that there is one universal God but do not believe that Jesus is the Son of God who lived, died, and was resurrected making eternal life available only through Him.[9] Buddhists look within to discover God, and Hindus stress the role of karma, neither acknowledging the divinity of Jesus as Lord through whom access and relationship with God are made available.[10] Certainly, this is not an exhaustive explanation of all religions

---

[7] Christopher Patridge, Introduction to World Religions (Minneapolis, MN: Fortress Press, 2018).

[8] Christopher Patridge, Introduction to World Religions (Minneapolis, MN: Fortress Press, 2018).

[9] Ibid.

[10] Ibid.

or the beliefs and tenets of those mentioned. The point is that a person's religion informs their foundational beliefs, adopted practices, and establishes traditions of faith. However, religion is something very different than a relationship.

It is possible to gain knowledge about religious doctrine and practices without experiencing a personal encounter or relationship with God. The study of God does not equate to being in a relationship with God. As a seminarian and avid reader of historical text, I had to learn that I must be careful not to allow my time of study to replace my time of worship and fellowship with God. The truth of the matter is that our quest to learn about God will always be incomplete, for our human limitations prevent us from fully understanding an omniscient, omnipotent, omnipresent God. However, we also know that studying to show thyself approved is of value. In fact, being knowledgeable about God and having a literacy of the Word of God is critically important to the strengthening of our faith. The problem arises when what we know does not transform how we live.

---

*The study of God does not equate to being in a relationship with God.*

---

Jesus spoke of those who were more concerned with being knowledgeable teachers of the law but had little concern for justice, mercy, and faithfulness. In the Gospel of Matthew Chapter 23, Jesus speaks to the teachers of the law and Pharisees and refers to them as "blind fools" because they thought their knowledge of God's laws were more important than living out the principles of God and demonstrating God's enormous love, grace, and compassion for all people. Their inability to place God's love above their sacred temples, ornamental regalia and fine possessions was a result of their lack of intimacy with God. Intimacy is an indication of relationship, one in which you spend personal and private time developing. You see, it is in the intimate moments with God that the Holy Spirit has the opportunity to reach the deepest places of our heart which allow for God's transforming power to conform us. If you have ever had an intimate encounter with God, you know that a person cannot experience God in this manner and remain unchanged. As recorded in the New Testament book of Acts, it was an encounter with God that changed everything for the Apostle Paul. A man who foolishly spent his life persecuting followers of Jesus is the same man whom God reveals as a chosen vessel to proclaim Jesus as Lord. It was through the Holy Spirit that God revealed to Paul that he had been foolish and removed the scales from Paul's eyes allowing him to finally see truth. This transformative encounter with God transcended beyond Paul's religious doctrine and blind zealousness. It was a turning point that changed the trajectory of his life, eventually writing over half of the New Testament! But, one can be so steeped in doctrine and traditions and completely miss having a transformative relationship with God. Religion alone is not enough to transform hearts and minds, an intimate encounter and relationship with God must be part of the experience.

This idea of having knowledge of religious doctrine without relationship was not only demonstrated during times of biblical antiquity. If we reflect on the inhumane history of slavery in the United States, we must acknowledge that Christianity was misused to justify devaluing African humanity and the resulting atrocities. Even more, it is said that Christian church services were held on the top level of the Elmina slave castle, located on the picturesque gold coast of West Africa in present day Ghana, while captive slaves lay on the bottom floor of the castle, naked, chained, and in their own defecation.[11] The "Christians" who were responsible for the Elmina castle and others like it were blinded of their collective moral failure, as they were unable to connect their proclaimed Christian doctrine to the value of African human lives.[12] It may seem inconceivable to most Christians today that there could be a line of delineation as to who the love of God applies to, but these Christians who misused religious doctrine for personal gain were blinded by the salacious catechism of greed and power. Unfortunately, if we take a careful look at the state of the Christian church in 2020, one might still be able to identify pockets of these schisms of the enemy at play.

---

[11] W. F. Conton, West Africa in History, Vol. I, Before 1800, (Allen & Unwin Academic, 2019).

[12] Richard Brown, The Door of No Return, Commonweal Magazine, May 8, 2017. Retrieved 7/28/2020, commonwealmagazine.org/door-no-return

I think it appropriate to discuss the role of the local church in our process of considering the distinctions of gaining religious knowledge, developing a relationship with God through Jesus Christ, and understanding that God stands alone. Our life-long journey of spiritual maturity and pursuit to live victoriously in God does not happen in isolation. Traditionally, the local church has been the organism that connects people together who share the same faith tradition. It has been the bedrock of many communities, particularly Black communities. Like many Christians, going to church is something that I have done for most all of my life. Although I did not come into a relationship with Jesus until an adult, my home church in Portsmouth, VA provided me with a foundation. If nothing else, I knew to seek God when my foolish attempts to live life without God inevitably failed ... miserably. I am grateful for an early exposure to the grounding of the Word of God through the church. I am also grateful for those individuals who've come before me committed to see the church not as divided but as a unifying organism of love and power.

But, there is a shift happening in how the local church functions and is perceived. With the technological developments of digital communication through sources such as Facebook Live, YouTube videos, and podcasts, many are deciding that being a part of a local assembly of believers is no longer necessary or important. I challenge this belief because it is based on the faulty thinking that we can accomplish all that God has created us to do without the help of others. This is a deception from the master deceiver, the devil, who often uses isolation as an entry point. Experience has proven that my personal spiritual growth is inextricably connected to being part of a body of believers. As 1 Corinthians 12:27 (NIV) informs us, "Now you are the body of Christ, and each one of you is a part of it."[13] We are reminded that as part of the body, we all have value, purpose, and must work together to function properly. Without being a part of a body of believers, no matter how well you are functioning individually, you limit your capabilities because your efforts are not in concert with others who need your gifts and you theirs. Don't be fooled by the lure of self-absorbed ambition but be drawn to the matchless love of God that causes us to reciprocate love, first towards God, yourself, and then to others.

The Covid-19 pandemic of 2020 has brought conversation about the local church to the forefront in many ecclesiastical circles. What happens when you *can't* go to church? The pandemic has forced Christians all over the world to answer this question, ironically at a time of crisis when people look to communities of faith for support. I believe that such a time as this is one where we must examine our personal relationship and experience with God. Do we have the personal faith to believe what we profess on Sunday morning? Can we still show up in the presence of God, absent of the church building? Sometimes we try to equate coming to the church building with the presence of God. But the question is never whether

---

[13] 1 Corinthians 12:12 - 31 compares the human body and all its many parts to the church, which is referred to the body of Christ.

God is present. God is omnipresent; here, there, and everywhere all at the same time. We must ask ourselves if *we* are fully present in our lives, with our spirit attuned to God. Perhaps God is concerned that we've learned how to have church service so well that some have missed a personal relationship with Him. I also believe that we should all be concerned when the Christian message stops at salvation and does not reach the practicality of daily living. The church must be concerned with the plight of those who are down-trodden, oppressed, and marginalized. Jesus' earthly ministry often touched those who were overlooked, ostracized, or cast aside, so we must also demonstrate this kind of love and value for those others devalue. Going to church is edifying but being the church is gratifying.

---

*Going to church is edifying but being the church is gratifying.*

---

I must emphasize that although the church is imperfect because it is comprised of imperfect people, the church is not an optional institution that can simply be dismantled because of human mishandling. It is implausible or at best a cataclysmic mistake to attempt to eliminate the institution of the church from Christianity. Jesus declared to Peter, who had proved himself as an imperfect servant, that "upon this rock I will build my church (Matthew 16:18, KJV)." Yet as a result of the implications of a trifecta of crises in America, we have suddenly encroached upon an opportune time to evaluate if we as the church are fulfilling our part in God's mission of salvation, *and* empowering people to see themselves as He sees us, *and* living accordingly through discipleship. Crisis has a way of sifting out what is most important from that which is preference. As a consequence of the Covid-19 pandemic, churches are re-evaluating what's essential and what really doesn't matter. All of a sudden, things like the color of ministry shirts or matching earrings for all the female ushers are not so important. There is a refocus on our reliance on God and the power of His Word. In the search for wisdom in times of uncertainty, let us remember that the beginning of wisdom is the fear of the Lord and only fools despise the wisdom of God (Proverbs 1:7, NKJV; Proverbs 9:10, NKJV). When you realize the magnificence and vastness of God, you must also recognize how incapable we are without a total dependence on His power.

It is not our religious doctrine, traditions, nor our ability to have church service as we've known it, that will sustain us in times of crisis. While these things have significance, it is our personal relationship with God through Jesus Christ and the realization that God alone is sovereign that will sustain us. We alone have limitations, but only God can stand alone as Almighty. God is self-sufficient, immutable, and timeless. Only God is Alpha and Omega, with full knowledge of the beginning and the end. The book of Revelation 1:8 (NKJV) says, "I am the Alpha and the Omega, the Beginning and the End" says the Lord, "who is, and who was, and who is to come, the Almighty." The dwelling place and knowledge of God is eternal and infinite but understanding of time is for humankind's measurement of the length of life on earth. God cannot be boxed into our human parameters nor our perceptions of one another. This is important to our understanding of our value in God and how, unlike people, God is able to see the totality of who we are created to be. This is good news for those who, as the Apostle Paul writes, "At one time we too were foolish, disobedient, deceived and enslaved by all kinds of passions and pleasures (Titus 3:3, NIV)." You must connect with your creator God, through Jesus Christ, in order to begin to understand the totality and uniqueness of the "you" God has created. Only God can introduce you to yourself. The closer you draw to God the more you begin to clearly see yourself. God alone has established who you are and all that he has purposed you to do.

The complication is that people are unable to see all that God intends to do through you. As a result, people have a tendency to try and place limitations on your future based upon how they have experienced life with you. If we are not careful, we can be fooled by other people's limited perception of who we are. What people seem to forget is that throughout the Bible, God used the unlikely, those who were looked over by people, and those with great flaws to accomplish His will. If we consider the life of King David, who was initially overlooked because of his small stature we can see how God defies the logic of humankind. When God sent the prophet Samuel to anoint

David as king, God reminded Samuel that, "the Lord sees not as man sees. Man looks at the outward appearance, but the Lord looks at the heart (1 Samuel 16:7, NKJV). Although people may overlook you because they are unable to see your divine potential, take heart beloved because God never overlooks us and has a divinely orchestrated purpose for our lives.

David is described as a man after God's own heart (1 Samuel 13:14, NKJV). Yet, David's life was not void of foolish errors. More importantly, God demonstrated faithfulness to forgive David when he repented for his sins. One of the amazing things about God it that God seems to specialize in taking that which seems inconceivable and using it for His glory. God will call a person to rise out of the deepest valleys to preach on the highest mountains. God will call a person from what appears to be a dry desolate place to produce and speak a wellspring of life. God will bring forth an innocuous person from the back and bring them to the front for His glory. As the Word of God says, "So the last will be first, and the first will be last (Matthew 20:16, NIV)". I can remember the response of some when I first began to preach the Gospel. My calling was a surprise to many, but not to God. As I wrestled with my imperfections and foolish mistakes from earlier points in my life, God reminded me that He was well aware of my inadequacy without Him when He called me and that the power that He has placed in me is greater than any insufficiency. I am so glad that it is God who is responsible for the qualifying! As 2 Corinthians 3:5 (NKJV) states, "Not that we are sufficient of ourselves to think of anything as being from ourselves, but our sufficiency is from God."[14] Be encouraged and know that with God, what's broken is made whole and what seems impossible becomes possible.

**Questions for your consideration ...**

1.  Reflect on your current understanding of religion, relationship with God, and God alone. How does your life demonstrate your understanding?

2.  What are your thoughts on being a part of the body of Christ? What do you need as a member of the body to function properly?

3.  How is the power of God evident in your life? What steps can you take to access the power of God that is within you?

---

[14] 2 Corinthians 3:5, New King James Version

# Prayer & Praise

Almighty God we seek your face. You are God and God alone. There is no one like you and I place no one and no thing above you. Thank you God for being my certainty in a time of uncertainty. Thank you for being my stability in times of instability. Help us to have the wisdom to know when to turn off the TV and take a break from the constant breaking news. Thank you for the wisdom to take time to turn my attention toward You and seek Your face. Father, I stand on your Word and trust that you are in control. In moments when I am struggling to trust or even to believe, I pray Father God that you will help my unbelief. I pray that in the midst of great challenge, I will see you high and lifted up. I pray that my faith may be increased. And finally I pray that as I draw closer to you Father, my eyes may be opened to new possibilities and my ears may be available to hear you speak into my future. Speak Lord. Holy Spirit, speak encouragement to my discouragement. Speak Lord healing to my brokenness. Speak Lord faith to my fear. Now God, we lift up the praise of Hallelujah for your love and grace. Hallelujah for the glory you have set before me. In the name of Jesus … Amen

## Chapter 3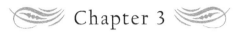

# It's Not Just You

---

The words fool, fools, foolish, foolishly, and foolishness appear in the Bible a combined total of 199 times.[15] That's good news because it gives us confidence that the issue of being a fool is not just a rare occurrence. When themes are repeated in the Bible, it is for emphasis and suggests that the writers wanted to be certain that an understanding is not missed. The frequency of the theme of "fool" and its derivatives makes a strong argument that God intends for readers of the Bible to pay attention to what is being said about this topic. Making foolish errors is not a contemporary phenomenon or something that is applicable only to a select few. We all have sinned and fall short of the glory of God (Romans 3:23, NKJV). While some may like to forget past errors, we must be careful that we never become so high in our spiritual

---

[15] The Bible, King James Version

walk with God that we no longer remember the grace that God has extended in our lives. Remembrance does not mean that we live life looking backwards, stuck in thoughts of what was and what happened. That will only stifle your forward progression and growth. Remembrance, however, should provide mental markers on your journey that allow you to measure how far you've come. Remembrance should also cause you to have compassion and patience with those who are still lost or spiritually blind. If we are able to be honest with ourselves, we must say that at one time or another, we have been foolish in our thoughts or actions. This acknowledgement does not mean you are weak or without value. Quite the opposite. It takes tremendous courage and strength to acknowledge error and effect change. Little faith is required to remain unchanged and to stay in destructive cycles.

---

*It takes tremendous courage and strength to acknowledge error and effect change. Little faith is required to remain unchanged and to stay in destructive cycles.*

---

The enemy has a way of trying to convince you that no one could possibly understand what you may have thought or done, that no one could understand your situation or circumstance. This is a lie that has deceived many. When you believe that you are the only one who has dealt with a particular struggle, it opens the door for shame and guilt to keep you in bondage to things that God wants you to be free from. The truth of the matter is that our humanity causes us to be susceptible to error, without the interventions of experience and engaging in a spiritual relationship with God. Even then, we are not immune to errors in judgement. We can acknowledge that there is a war that rages between the threat of our old ways of thinking and doing, with our new mind. Our carnal mind and the Spirit of God that lives in us are in contrast with one another, meaning we must make a committed effort to be led by the Spirit (Galatians 5:17–18, NIV). We are in a life-long process of spiritual formation which suggests that there is a part of each of us that is still being transformed. Salvation does not mean that we will never make a mistake or that we are immediately transformed into the likeness of Jesus. Salvation is the security of eternal life, but spiritual transformation is a life-long process. God often uses life experiences as teachable moments of correction. God does not simply dispose of our errors, but uses them for His glory when we come into an understanding of our foolish mistakes and decide that God's ways are greater than our own.

---

*Salvation is the security of eternal life, but spiritual transformation is a life-long process.*

---

The errors in our ways of thinking and doing are not confined to one area of life, but we can recognize that relationships are frequently the platform where our foolish mistakes manifest. This is not by happenstance. As mentioned in the previous chapter, we are created to be communal. It is not God's intention that we accomplish His will alone. We partner with God and we partner with people. We are co-laborers with God to accomplish His will. Our character and spiritual discipline is developed through connectivity with other people. By God's design, we are to function in a relationship with Him first and then in relationship with others. A challenge for many of us is determining who to be in a relationship with, the type of relationship, and whether the relationship is seasonal or permanent. Confusing any of the three will undoubtedly lead to difficulty and sets the stage for a tailor-made learning experience. The enemy is aware of your areas of vulnerability and will seek a foothold. As stated in Proverbs 13:20 (NRSV), "Whoever walks with the wise becomes wise, but the companion of fools suffers harm". But God's omniscience is able to limit the level of struggle to that which is needed for you to come into the actualization of your potential. I will talk about this more in Chapter 6, but please know that struggle is a necessary part of any process of growth including our spiritual growth. A simple illustration of this is the story of the butterfly that left the cocoon too soon.[16] As the caterpillar was being transformed in the cocoon into a butterfly, a young boy noticed the butterfly was struggling to get out of the cocoon and decided to create

---

[16] http://instructor.mstc.edu/instructor/swallerm/Struggle%20-%20Butterfly. htm#:~:text=Every%20day%20he%20watched%20the,it%20new%20plants%20 to%20eat.&text=The%20boy%20worriedly%20called%20his,metamorphosis%20 and%20become%20a%20butterfly.

a hole so that the butterfly did not have to struggle and could have an easier exit. What the young boy did not realize was that the butterfly's struggle to get out of the cocoon was necessary to build up the strength of its wings in order to fly properly. But because the process of transformation was short-circuited and the process of struggle was lightened, once the butterfly was released from the cocoon it was unable to fly because it did not have the necessary strength in its wings. Instead of trying to escape from struggle, allow God to use the struggle to develop your strength. The victory that believers can stand upon is that what the devil intends for evil, God intends for our good. The devil is intent to steal, kill, and destroy you before you come into an awareness of who you are in God. God's intent is to transform you into the likeness of Jesus-Christ so that you may live a victorious life.

When it comes to relationships, there are two insights that God has given me and are worthy of our discussion as we consider foolish errors. The first is that we should evaluate the potentiality of any relationship based on God's standards and not solely on our desired outcomes or needs. When we seek God for guidance and receive His wisdom through the Holy Spirit, we are less likely to find ourselves out of position for what God has for our lives. I spent years in relationships with people who were not a part of God's plan for my future. I was blinded by a misdirected desire for love. Not only did I allow the wrong people in, each time, I placed people in a position of expectation that only God can occupy. There is a love that only

God can provide. When we place an expectation on people to provide the love that only God is capable of providing, we are bound to be disappointed. This is yet another reason why our relationship with God is so important. God's wisdom is only accessible through His Spirit, which dwells in those who are in relationship with Him. Also, a relationship with God gives us the grounding to trust God beyond what our human eyes can see. When we do not seek God's guidance for our relationships with others, we tend to make decisions based on what we see at the time. But God is able to see far beyond the current moment in time and knows all that each of us will become. It is written that, "What no eye has seen, what no ear has heard, and what no human mind has conceived all the things God has prepared for those who love Him."[17] These things that are unseen and unheard are only revealed through the Holy Spirit. Be careful not to disqualify those from your life that do not appear to fit and meet your every preference. Let God be the judge and follow the guidance of His Holy Spirit.

The second insight is that God may be waiting on you to take a step of obedience. All of the answers may not be clear, but there may be one thing that God is waiting on you to do. If you find yourself in a place where you are tired of dealing with the same foolishness and making the same foolish errors, it may be that there is a step of obedience that God is waiting on you to take. God will allow us to repeat experiences until we make the necessary change. Partners may change, locations

---

[17] 1 Corinthians 2:9, New International Version

may change, jobs may change, but the constant is you. The danger of this cycle is that you may not be able to see your error until it's over and you've endured yet another injury. After divorce and navigating through life as a single parent of three young sons, I had to come to the understanding that what God was requiring of me was much more than how I operated prior to professing my life to Jesus Christ. If I was going to survive and expose my sons to a life that dared them to be the best versions of themselves, I had to seek a source that was greater than myself. That source was God, who proved to be the source of every resource that I needed. From the moment I entered into a covenant relationship with God through Jesus Christ, old ways of doing life were no longer effective. How I entered into my first marriage was not how God would allow me to enter into a second marriage, now that I had experienced a rebirth. The step of obedience that God required of me was a period of celibacy, in which I finally made God my first love and priority.

This is not a decision that I came to easily. Isn't it incredible how we will fight against God's wisdom and hold on to familiar foolish ways of doing things, even when those things lead to repetitive injuries. I was resistant and stubborn until I reached the point of emotional and psychological breaking. It was at my breaking point that I fully and completely surrendered my will to God and I began to hear the clarity of God's voice. God began to reveal to me that from the point of violation as a teenage girl, I had been searching for a love in people that only He could provide. Once I surrendered the fullness of my heart to God, in the quietness of my spirit God whispered to me that my search was over. This was a time of purification and preparation. Soon after, the man whom God selected to be my husband came into my life and brought with him a love that is a gift from God. God allowed me to fail in my own foolishness until I finally decided to trust Him with this portion of my life. Sometimes, we trust God in most areas but leave one area that we think we can handle on our own and in our own way. I am a witness that this strategy is a grave mistake and comes from the deception of the enemy. We are to trust God with our whole heart! As Proverbs 3:5 (NIV) informs us, "Trust in the Lord with all your heart and lean not on your own understanding." To leave a portion of your heart uncovered is to make space for the enemy's deception.

For every strategy of deception that the enemy uses to lure us into foolish ways of thinking and doing, we must have a counter-response that is greater. This response is found in the Word of God. It is the Word of God that provides the solid foundation that can stand up against the schemes of the enemy. Only the fool builds a foundation on the shakiness of sand, which shifts and sways as storms arise (Matthew 7:26, NIV). A shaky foundation of sand is unstable because it changes with the wind. If our foundational beliefs in God change whenever life gets difficult, the instability will expose what we really believe and place our hope and faith in.

When I was a new believer, many could tell me what and where but few could answer the question of how. I needed to know how to live a victorious life now that I had overcome so much. I needed to know how to handle new challenges without reverting back to old ways. The questions became, "what do I do when what I once did no longer works?", "How do I operate as a new creature, especially when my external circumstances have not changed?". You are experiencing God's transforming power inside of you, but you are having to learn how the new you can change the atmosphere in an old place. The second half of the book will discuss how to handle life as a believer, after overcoming failures and foolish mistakes, and through future troubles. I will share how I have learned to live in my "Now What." Hopefully, these strategies will help you to grow spiritually and cause you to walk boldly towards your greatest potential with your confidence in God.

**Questions for your consideration ...**

1. What area(s) of your life are you holding on to and attempting to handle without God?

2. Reflect on the relationships in your life. Is it time to re-evaluate who you are in a relationship with, the type of relationship, and whether the relationship is seasonal or permanent?

3. What step of obedience has God spoken into your spirit that you have not taken yet?

# Prayer & Praise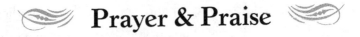

Father God, thank you for your unshakeable unfailing love. A love that covered and protected me even when I couldn't see that I needed protection. I thank you for keeping me despite my foolish heart until I learned to turn my heart towards you. Help me Lord to surrender the foolishness in me to your transforming power. As I walk on my journey with you Lord, help me to know who to connect with, who to enter in covenant with, and who to move away from. I trust you Lord to order my steps and I will be faithful to stand up and take one obedient step at a time. Oh God of my salvation, I intentionally frustrate the enemy and praise you with gladness because I am still here, still able to live my best life yet. I praise you God for your divine strategy and being my fortress and keeping the cords of death from entangling me. I call on you Lord God because you hear my prayer and are worthy of all honor and praise. In the inimitable name of Jesus. Amen.

# PART 2

*Renewal, Reshaping,
and Rebranding*

##  Chapter 4

# Replacing Old Thoughts

Whenever we make a decision to move away from foolish behaviors that are unproductive or behaviors that are out of God's will for our lives, there is a void that must be filled. This state of vulnerability is where the enemy will often attack if we are not careful to fill this space with thoughts and habits that honor God. If not, you may find that you have simply traded one unproductive behavior or habit for another. When embarking on any journey, it is wise to seek guidance from a reliable source. As a believer, your reliable source is God the Father and He has provided the Word of God as our guide, and the Holy Spirit as our power to accomplish that which the Word reveals.

Replacing our old thoughts involves the internal engrafting of the Word of God into our heart and mind (James 1:21, KJV). The idea of engrafting means that the Word of God becomes an integral part of our being, connecting with God spirit to spirit, and producing an irreplaceable hope. It's when the connection with God through His Word becomes a part of our daily condition. Some have naively attempted to reduce the Word of God to an optional source. Such deception is from the enemy and only works to strip the believer of the power gained by being rooting in truth. Understand, the adversary knows that once the Word of God is planted and rooted in you, you are a threat to his schemes. When the Word of God is engrafted in you it will stand up to every lie of the enemy. The last thing the enemy wants is for you to get a hold of the Word in your heart and mind. When we are able to receive the Word fully and completely, without the barriers of pride and fear, we make space for the Word of God to become active in our lives. When we place our thoughts on the Word of God, our life begins to look like that which we focus our thoughts on. The Bible provides this guidance, "whatever is true, whatever is honorable, whatever is just, whatever is pure, whatever is lovely, whatever is commendable, if there is any excellence, if there is anything worthy of praise, think about these things" (Philippians 4:8, ESV).

---

*When the Word of God is engrafted in you it will stand up to every lie of the enemy.*

---

There are those who like to point out historical inconsistencies within the biblical text or debate the authorship of biblical writings. I have found that many of these debates are distractions and can cause us to miss what God wants to reveal. I don't know about you, but I have discovered that I do not have time to engage in fruitless conversations of doubt when I have a struggle to fight and a divine potential to reach. Such discussions are intellectual exercises that have limitations and more importantly, do not negate the biblical truths and principles that we are to live by. As you strive to replace your thoughts, do not be distracted by inconsequential facts that are irrelevant to truth.

For many, our minds are bombarded by distractions and the constant noise of our lives. Distractions show up not only as concerns but also as blessings. If we allow our blessings to overshadow the God who blessed us, we will choke our growth and hinder our maturity and may forfeit the fullness of what God has for us. Be careful not to mistake the singular blessing for the harvest, when God is saying He's not finished with you yet. This is why our intentionality for transformation must extend beyond the salvation moment. If we stop at salvation, we short circuit the fullness of what God wants to do through us. The life we live beyond salvation is how we honor God and experience the benefits of the Kingdom of God on earth.

Being able to replace our old thoughts does not happen just by attending church service once a week. It is going to take some work. It's taken years of your life to develop the ways of thinking and doing that you now desire to break. Change begins with a moment but is not void of process. It takes intentionality to resist the appetite for immediacy, in a world driven by convenience and the illusion of fulfillment through obtaining more of the tangible. We must be careful not to fall into a consumerist Christianity, where the focus is on what we can receive without any effort towards personal growth and accountability. The Word of God was not provided just for our consumption without action or change. It is not simply for our listening pleasure. Yes, faith does come by hearing and hearing by the Word of God (Romans 10:17, NKJV). But also, faith without works is dead (James 2:17, NKJV). Our ability to replace our old thoughts requires us to come into the knowledge and understanding of the Word of God through the discipline of study. Setting aside time to read your Bible and commune with God is where we engage in an intimacy that increases our ability to respond to life differently and in a way that reflects the spirit of God within. It's a personal relationship. We have a choice in what we decide to focus our thoughts on. We have a choice in what thoughts we hold on to and give life to. Sometimes it's easy to give negative thoughts legs, feet, and wings and allow those thoughts to take off down a fruitless path only to later find out that you were incorrect and operating based on past experiences. We can't hold the people in our present and future, hostage to the traumas of our past. Doing so can sabotage the very blessing God has provided in your life. Instead, Godly wisdom will allow you to pause, seek the Holy Spirit for guidance, and then determine if your thought commends life or death. We can decide on the thoughts that we need to cancel and replace. I tell you, God is concerned with our thought life. God is concerned with what we allow our mind to meditate on. This is why 2 Corinthians 10:5 (NIV) reminds us of our ability to "take captive of every thought." This only happens with intention. One way that we take captive or take hold of our thoughts is by meditating on the Word of God, instead of meditating on that which is against God.

Your pastor's faith cannot substitute for your personal relationship and intimacy with God. Sometimes I think we forget that our pastors are real human beings with real issues of life to deal with in addition to being God's chosen shepherd of a particular people. We cannot continue to exalt our pastors and clergy to a seat of sovereignty that only God can occupy. Doing so, gives the false indication that the layperson does not have to seek God for themselves which weakens the body of believers and the local church. I now know what the old saints meant when they would say, "You can't live off of mama's faith, you've got to know God for yourself!" The power that you desire to walk in will require your faith, commitment, and participation as the Holy Spirit works through the Word of God to transform your life from the inside out.

Jesus describes the Word of God as analogous to a seed.[18] Like a seed, in order for us to develop into all that God has hidden in us we must go through a process of transformation, a stage of being uncomfortable, growing from one level to the next, coming outside of one's comfort zone, expanding beyond the confinements of infancy, so that we may grow towards maturity. Also like a seed,

---

[18] Parable of the Sower and the Seed, Luke 8:4-15

the word of God must be planted in our heart and mind in order to become active in our life. The ability for the seed to grow is dependent upon the condition of the ground. Like so, the spiritual condition of our heart can influence whether or not the Word of God becomes rooted. The richest soil includes matter that has decomposed, meaning something that died is used as part of the process of creating a stronger environment for the seed to grow. When old things pass away and we become a new creature through our rebirth in Jesus, this literally means that there are things in our lives that must spiritually die in order for us to walk in our newness. Not only must these things die, there is a process of decomposition that slowly strengthens us by using the substance of what once threatened to destroy us, for a new purpose. The threats become opportunities to exercise our faith, which the Bible describes as the substance of things hoped for. This transformative process is a slow process that can be frustrating and cause you to wonder if it's really worth it. But if you can endure the process with God, you will find that on the other side of your frustration is strength like you've never known. "Consider that our present sufferings are not even worth comparing with the glory that will be revealed in us" (Romans 8:18, NIV).

We often look at other people and see God's glory through their lives, but fail to understand that there was a process before the glory was revealed. This is why it is unwise to be envious of those who walk in great anointing and power. There is an equally great process and sacrifice that has preceded the strength that is on display for the world to see. This is how God takes all things that have happened, the good and the bad, and works them together for good for those who love Him and are called according to his purpose (Romans 8:28, NIV). Yes, you have a call and you have a purpose. These are benefits of being a child of God and joint heir with Jesus Christ. So often, we place an exclusionary meaning on the word "call" as if it only applies to clergy. You are called and have purpose because you belong to God. The called includes every true believer. Are you a true believer? No really, are you a true believer? As true believers we are called to live a life that honors God. We are called to be servants of God, not to a casual Christianity. And because we are called, we can be certain that God has a specific purpose for our lives. We are not here by happenstance. God has kept you and is keeping you on purpose for a purpose. Not only are we called, but we are also chosen as God's special possession, that because of the blood of Jesus you may declare the praises of him who called you out of darkness into his wonderful light. Praise God! No matter what the circumstances were that resulted in your conception. God allowed you to enter into this world because of God's plan for your life. Some of you reading this book may have been conceived in a one night stand, or through an adulterous relationship, or even the result of rape or incest. Those circumstances do not revoke God's promise on your life for a glorious hope and a rich future in Him.

---

*You are called and have purpose because you*
*belong to God.*

---

47

In the early years of my walk with God, I learned to encourage myself by speaking the Word of God out loud. This articulation helped me in reinforcing my convictions but also it put the enemy on notice that I am not falling for the same schemes any longer. When I would feel tired and overwhelmed by life's challenges, I would remind myself to stay the course by speaking Galatians 5:1 (NKJV), "Stand fast therefore in the liberty by which Christ has set me free and do not be entangled again in the yoke of bondage." This scripture would anchor my thoughts when I felt tempted to revert back to the old. When I would feel defeated by disappointments, I would remind myself of who God says that I am by referring to the scriptures I shared in the affirmations listed in chapter one. Then I learned about the armor of God in Ephesians and how to use these spiritual weapons to win the battles of life, realizing that the battle we often fight is internal and it is spiritual. The spiritual part of me that is surrendered to God, battles with the flesh that is still being disciplined and transformed. I gained an understanding that we fight not against people, but against spiritual forces of wickedness and a hierarchy of evil. For our struggle is not against flesh and blood, but against the rulers, against the authorities, against the powers of this dark world and against the spiritual forces of evil in the heavenly realms. Therefore put on the full armor of God, so that when the day of evil comes, you may be able to stand your ground, and after you have done everything, to stand. (Ephesians 6:12–13, NIV)

When you understand that the battles we fight are both

spiritual and within, you can understand that your response must also be spiritual. We accomplish much through prayer and it is the medium that connects us to the power and protection of our Father God. Throughout the Bible, the right hand of God is a symbol of power and protection. It is God's right hand that shatters the enemy. It is our Lord and Savior Jesus Christ who is seated at the right hand of our God interceding in prayer for us. I'm not sure if you heard that … Jesus is interceding for you at the right hand of God and it is the right hand of God that will uphold you. That's powerful! Whenever fear attempts to invade your thoughts during times of uncertainty, we can replace our fear with faith knowing that Jesus is seated at the right hand of God interceding in prayer on our behalf. It is just as powerful to consider that we personally have access to come boldly to the throne of God in prayer because of the reconciliation made possible through Jesus. Through our personal relationship with Jesus Christ, we have access to spiritual weapons that allow us to victoriously stand against the wiles of the devil. Prayer, the Word of God which is our sword, and praise work intricately together through the Holy Spirit to give us strength through every battle and the endurance to stand even when you do not feel like standing.

Learning to replace old ways of thinking and doing with the Word of God is not a seamless straight-line process. There will be much to learn on the path as you make uncomfortable adjustments. It involves days when you will struggle to get it right. But as you continue with your transformative process, you will be strengthened and there will be more days that you walk in power and fewer days of weary. The important piece is to keep going, keep showing up, and never ever quit. As a believer, quitting is no longer your option. You may have moments when you feel like quitting, but take comfort in knowing that God is with you in those moments and is pulling for you to remember His love and grace. It is in these moments where God will prove that His strength is made perfect in your weakness. Our perfection is not the requirement in order to experience the promises of God. In the next chapter, we will talk about what is.

**Questions for your consideration …**

1.  How will you work to strengthen your walk with God and your ability to live a victorious life?

2.  Reflect on your response to life during times that required you to be uncomfortable during your process of transformation. What steps will you take to keep moving forward?

3.  Reflect on your thought life? Are there more thoughts of defeat or victory? How will you take captive of your thoughts?

#  Prayer & Praise

Gracious God, thank you for the gift of the opportunity to renew our mind today. You, Father God, are my strength and You have given me the ability to choose the thoughts that I give life to. Help me to choose wisely. Help me to take captive of those thoughts that do not speak life and replace those thoughts with Your Word of truth. Mighty God, help me to pull down strongholds and any thought that threatens to steal, kill, or destroy me. When I am uncomfortable in my process, I will place my trust in You. Some trust in chariots and some in horses, but I trust in You Lord. I sing praises to Your name God. I praise You for the victory and the glory that is being revealed. In the name of Jesus. Amen.

# Chapter 5

# Perfection Is Not The Requirement, So What Is?

There is a prevalent misconception that being a Christian means that you should be able to live a life without ever sinning, either sins of omission or commission. Some have the idea that once you become a Christian you will be able to live a perfect life. Those who have this idea will quickly tout things like "I thought you were a Christian" when you err or do not live up to their standard of perfection. Not only does this paint an inaccurate picture of the Christian life, it places an undo level of pressure on Christians to be perfect finished products. This unrealistic expectation causes some to feel as though they can never live up to such perfection and actually pushes people away from the faith because there is a constant feeling of not being good enough. While you are trying to figure out why you can't seem to live up to this perfect idealism, often the people who are promoting this idea have failed to tell you that they can't either. They too have areas of weakness and struggle. They fail to tell you that what you perceive of them is an incomplete picture, only a fraction of their reality. Or perhaps, they may not let you in on the fact that they haven't always been the person you see today. I chuckle to myself sometimes because people who have only known me since I've walked with God cannot seem to imagine that I could have been a different person. What they see is the glory of God in an imperfect vessel. Many Christians emphasize that they are not Jesus and are not perfect when attempting to explain some human proclivity or offense. It is correct that we are not perfect beings, but we do have access to a perfect Holy Spirit who is able to assist us in our human condition.

There is an equally prevalent misconception that God only desires our salvation and does not require us to change. These are those who feel as though as long as they have the security of salvation, they can live life on their own terms with little regard for the principles of God. The common explanations are offered through statements like "God knows my heart" or "God knows where I am", as if this acknowledgment excuses their disregard for God's requirements of those who profess Jesus as Lord and Savior. God's grace is not to be taken for granted. There are responsibilities that come with gaining the knowledge of who God is and who you are in God. Once you know, you really can't live life the same and in constant disobedience without being convicted by the Holy Spirit. You can certainly try, but it's been my experience that God's correction in our lives is often much more disruptive than when we are able to heed to the warning signs and come into our own realization that change is needed.

Leaning on either of these misconceptions will prevent you from reaching your full potential in God and rob you of the abundant life that Jesus came to provide. The truth is that when we are in a personal relationship with God through Jesus Christ, the Holy Spirit is able to assist in continually conforming us towards the likeness of Christ. This is a lifelong process of growth and maturity, with us growing from faith to greater levels of faith and glory to greater glory of God through our lives. But this process does not happen without our active participation and intentional decisions. We do not sit on the outskirts of our life as an observer while God does everything. As a co-laborer in our process of transformation, we must intentionally seek God continually. I believe this is the intention of the familiar scripture in 1 Thessalonians 5:17 (NKJV), to pray without ceasing. The Greek words translated to pray without ceasing are *proseuchomai adialeiptos*, literally meaning to pray without omission, to intentionally have a constant awareness and sensitivity to God's voice and listening ear in all matters.[19] The closer we intentionally draw to God, the more

---

[19] *Strong's Exhaustive Concordance: New American Standard Bible.* 1995. Updated ed. La Habra: Lockman Foundation. http://www.biblestudytools.com/concordances/strongs-exhaustive-concordance/

our will begins to align with God's will for our lives. As a result, our lives should demonstrate some evidence of our relationship with God.

---

*What God requires is our belief, love, and obedience.*

---

What God requires is our belief, love, and obedience. Our personal relationship with God begins with our decision to believe that He is the one and only true and living God, the I am, the Almighty who is the creator of the universe. When we enter into a relationship with God through Jesus Christ, we are professing that we believe Jesus to be the son of God and accept Him as the only Lord and Savior of our life. Everything that proceeds from that point on, hinges on our faith to believe. As we journey through life, we discover that our faith to believe will be tested through situations and circumstances. For example, if you are in need of healing you must actually believe that God is able to heal you. There is a story in the ninth chapter of the gospel of Mark that speaks to the quandary that we often find ourselves in. We profess to believe God, yet we must confess that there are moments during times of testing that we need help with our unbelief. When Jesus arrives to heal a child that his disciples were unsuccessful in healing, he tells the child's father that in essence if he can believe, all things are possible. The father's response was "Lord, I believe. Help my unbelief!" I love this response because it reveals our duality of how we can be strong in confessing our belief in one area juxtaposed with how we must face our crisis of unbelief during times of great testing. It is in these moments that we must decide if we have the faith to believe that God is God and can do what seems impossible, despite the particulars of your circumstances that you see.

I submit that we really do not know what we believe until we have to stand on our beliefs and demonstrate our faith. It's easy to *say* that we believe. But it is in times of testing that our belief is revealed and our faith is purified. Testing does not always look like times of trouble. I've learned that testing can show up during times of walking in great blessings. We must be diligent to not allow what God has blessed us to accomplish to dampen our reliance on God. Our belief must remain resolute and our faith focused on the glory of God. We cannot become so comfortable in our relationship with God that we forget that in the twinkling of an eye, all that has been attained on earth can be lost. Our belief and our faith must remain fixed on those things that are eternal, understanding that our earthly treasures are temporal. Our belief and our faith are closely linked together but are not necessarily one in the same. Our belief speaks to what we value as being truth, and our faith is the action that accompanies our belief. For example, my belief is that all things are possible with God. But my faith, therefore, is the action of intentionally seeking God for what seems impossible *because* I believe all things are possible with God. My belief is that God loves me and sent His son Jesus to die on my behalf. My faith, therefore, is the action of making God my first love and loving God with my whole heart *because* I believe that God loves me and sent His only begotten son to save me. I think you get the point.

The primary message that is revealed through the life, death, and resurrection of Jesus Christ is the love that God has for us. In turn, God has left us with a requirement or commandment to love. This requirement was spoken by Jesus and recorded in each of the synoptic gospels. Mark, believed by many modern theologians to be the oldest gospel writer, says it like this. "Love the Lord your God with all your heart and with all your soul and with all your mind and with all your strength. The second is this: Love your neighbor as yourself. There is no commandment greater than these." (Mark 12:28-31, NIV) I cannot emphasize these words enough as I try to convey strategies for walking in your "Now What". Please take notice of the repetition of the word all. Not part of your heart, soul, mind, and strength, but all. This first sentence is a complete surrender and yielding to loving God. It teaches us that our love for God is our first priority. All the love that we have for ourselves and others must begin with our love for God. When we get this out of order and place our love for ourselves or others above our love for God, we will experience difficulty. This is because only God is the sustainer of life and provides us with the only trustworthy safe space for our total being. Proper divine order allows the Holy Spirit to produce the fruit of love in us that is like-minded with the love of God. To place anything or anyone above God is like trying to walk with power but exclude the source, and yet wonder why it's not working.

---

*To place anything or anyone above God is like trying to walk with power but exclude the source, and yet wonder why it's not working.*

---

The second part of this requirement is to love others (neighbors) as we love ourselves. The intention of the word neighbors is not limited to those who live in close proximity, or to those we like and are familiar with, or to our family members. It does not exclude those of different ethnicities, cultures, or who have a different faith tradition. It does not leave out your enemies or those who are against you. The word neighbor is an inclusive word that has very little to do with how we feel about others. It is based on the knowledge of who God is, who we are created to be, and our decision to live a life that pleases Him. The Greek word *agape'* is the word that is used in this scripture and translated in the English as love. In line with how agape was used during biblical times, this type of love is based on morality, not on emotion or superficial appearance.[20] It is a verb, an action word that requires demonstration. So loving others cannot just be lip service, even when it's not our preference. Again, we can be ever so thankful that we have the Holy Spirit to assist. When we find it difficult to love those who have injured us or come against us, it is the Holy Spirit that is

---

[20] https://www.preceptaustin.org/love-agape

able to remind us of the enormous unfailing unconditional love that God has shown us. Recalling God's demonstration of love in our lives helps to perceive that when we love others, this is actually our demonstration of love and honor towards God. It is God's demonstration of love and the transforming power of the Holy Spirit that motivates us to want to live an obedient life that glorifies God. This is our response when we truly realize what God has done for us. When we are no longer walking as blind fools and can see truth, it causes us to want to honor God with our lives and do better.

Obedience is not a popular word in the contemporary church of the 21st century but it is still relevant in order for us to move from glory to glory. Please do not misinterpret obedience for perfection. Being obedient means to make every human effort to do what God has said for our lives and in doing so we glorify God. That is our responsibility. The Holy Spirit helps us in our effort to accomplish this great task. But that does not mean that we will not struggle or that we will not fail at times. Failure can be the very thing that produces the perseverance and character that readies us for the next blessing. The Bible provides an excellent illustration for our consideration through the story of Peter and Jesus walking on the water. As Jesus walked on the water, Jesus responded to Peter's fear by inviting him to simply, come. "And when Peter had come down out of the boat, he walked on the water to go to Jesus. But when he saw that the wind was boisterous, he was afraid; and beginning to sink he cried out, saying, "Lord, save me!" And immediately

Jesus stretched out His hand and caught him, and said to him, "O you of little faith, why did you doubt?" And when they got into the boat, the wind ceased" (Matthew 14:28–32, NKJV). Peter's initial step to get out of the boat while the other disciples remained in the boat was a step of obedience. What's interesting in this story is that the wind does not become boisterous until Peter steps out of the boat. Sometimes, it seems that things get crazy after taking a step of obedience towards God because the enemy wants you to lose focus. But God will prove himself faithful in our lives. The moment that Peter gets scared and doubts, he instinctively cries out to the Lord Jesus who was faithful to immediately catch him. We must not forget the moments that we started to fall only to realize that we were falling into God's loving arms. Yes, for a moment Peter looked down and took His eyes off of God, but it was the trouble that caused him to refocus his eyes back on the Lord. Trouble has a way of causing us to refocus our eyes on what matters most. It has a way of causing us to see where our help comes from. Trouble has a way of pushing us to pray. Peter prayed, Lord, save me! Not a wordy prayer but an effective prayer that caused an immediate move of God.

I believe that the Peter who returned to the boat with Jesus had a greater faith because of his personal encounter with God. And when it is all said and done, after the wind dies down, those who are watching from afar will know that you've been with God. The story concludes by letting us know that those who were still in the boat, watching the whole thing, started worshipping God after seeing Peter's process. There are people who are watching you and your process. It's not just about our individual focus. There are people who may be drawn to God because of what they see God doing in our lives. There are people whose deliverance and salvation may be tied to your step of obedience. And please notice … it's not about perfection. It is about taking steps of obedience and being able to refocus on God when we get it wrong. It's about growing from one level of faith to another. In the midst of all that is happening in the world, it can be challenging to keep our focus on God. As we deal with the boisterous winds of things like personal illness, family death, or financial struggle it's easy to become more focused on the wind than on the Lord who has said "Come". But the beauty of it is that we serve a God who will immediately catch us and allow us to refocus our eyes on Him. We must remember that whatever the boisterous wind is that blows in our lives, it is Jesus who can calm the wind. It is Jesus who, at a Word, calms the wind and says peace be still. Remember that there is no wind that is blowing in your life right now that Jesus cannot calm. On today, I urge you to make a commitment to focus your attention on God and if need be refocus your attention on God. He is the one and only, who is forever faithful and true.

Obedience also means we are intentional to continue in our press even when we get it wrong. Obedience and perfection are not one in the same. Like the Apostle Paul, "Not that I have already obtained this or am already perfect, but I press on to make it my own, because Christ Jesus has made me his own."

When we profess that Jesus is Lord of our lives, this means that our life should demonstrate his Lordship. Jesus asked the people, "Why do you call me, 'Lord, Lord,' and do not do what I say? His point in asking the question was to show that their obedience to His words was for their benefit. Our obedience is not for God, it is for us. Obedience is the wisdom that God offers us through our reverence of Him and it is only the fool who rejects the knowledge of God's wisdom (Proverbs 1:7, NIV). This is important for our understanding because the wisdom of God is pure, peace giving, and fruit bearing (James 3:17, NIV). This means that our obedience is profitable for our lives.

Some may argue that God does not require our obedience because he has given us free will. But I challenge that if we intend to live life in the fullness of what God has for each of us, our obedience will be necessary. One reason we have difficulty with obedience is because we are driven by our senses and compare our lives to others. When we are more led by what we see and feel instead of the truth that we know, we can be deceived and fall into disobedience. It may seem that the disobedient are prospering and the faithful are suffering, and that God has forgotten that you are waiting. Beloved, it is in these moments when we must remember that it is only God who is omniscient. There are blessings that await you on the other side of your steps of obedience that are greater than you can imagine. There are blessings that are inaccessible and will not be revealed until you begin to obey what God has spoken directly to you. The beauty is that we serve a patient God, whose love extends beyond our procrastination, doubts, and fears. We do not have to have everything figured out. God walks with us step by step. When my sons were young one of their favorite books that I would read to them was called Step by Step.[21] The story was about the steps of the ant, steps that seemed small but were deliberate. Step by step the ant crossed a stone and then another stone. The ant kept his eye focused forward and on the main thing with every deliberate step, eventually crossing the stones that were in its path. When we keep our eyes focused forward and on God as our main thing while taking deliberate steps of obedience, we overcome the obstacles on our path step by step. Take a step of obedience and watch God meet you right where you are and guide you towards greater.

**Questions to consider ...**

1. What are some specific examples of how your faith demonstrates your belief in God?

2. In what area is God requiring you to take a step of obedience in faith? What is hindering your steps? What is motivating your steps?

3. There is nothing that compares to the love of God. When you think about God's love for you, what comes to mind? How is God's love demonstrated in your life?

---

[21] Diane Wolkstein, Step by Step (New York: Morrow Junior Books, 1994).

# Prayer & Praise

Father God, I believe you are the only true and living God. I believe that you sent your son Jesus to die and be resurrected so that I will be saved. Father God, I believe every promise that You have spoken over my life. Thank you Lord for the love you have for me and I surrender my heart, soul, and mind to you. Lord, I have decided to love my neighbor as myself. I have decided that Your ways are better than my ways. Thank you Lord for your strength and grace with every step. Thank you, Lord, for the wisdom to keep trusting You even when I can't see the total path. Lord God, I give You praise as I am being transformed into your image from glory to glory. I praise you God, not because of how I feel, but because of who You are. I praise You Lord with the essence of who I am and with gratitude for who I am becoming in You God. In the name of Jesus. Amen.

# Chapter 6

# The Truth About Trouble: It Is Necessary

Being a believer of Jesus Christ as Lord and Savior does not exempt us from trouble or difficult circumstances. Quite honestly, there are moments and seasons as a believer that it may seem as though you experience more trouble. It is these moments and seasons that have taught me that God is my help, strength, and refuge. God will prove that He is your present help in times of trouble. You only understand God's strength in your life when trouble causes you to realize that your strength alone is not enough. You only understand God to be a refuge when trouble doesn't go away, when difficult circumstances do not change, or when you have to endure death-like experiences and you find safety in God's love. Some of you were born into troublesome situations or experienced trouble or trauma at an early age that was no fault of your own.

But God has a way of giving us great beauty for our ashes and great anointing for great trouble. He will not scrap even your most traumatic experiences but will use it for good. Then there are other times when trouble shows up in our lives as the natural consequence of our disobedience. Even in these moments, God's grace remains sufficient. The consequences could have been worse, should have been worse, but God's grace steps in to reassure us that He is still in control.

In any of these realities, we can have confidence in knowing that there is no amount of trouble that God cannot see us through. This does not mean that God will always make the trouble go away or grant the outcome that we desire. But God is able to see us through the most challenging circumstances of life and will take what was intended to harm us and use it for good. We must remember that our experience with trouble is not God's first experience with trouble. As it is written in 1 Peter 4:12 (KJV), "Beloved, think it not strange concerning the fiery trial which is to try you, as though some strange thing happened unto you." What feels unique and uncommon to us is very familiar to God. Understanding this allows us to place our hope and faith in God, despite what any given situation may look like. As believers, we have bold access to God the Father who loves us unconditionally and who promises to never leave nor forsake us. My times of foolish mistakes have taught me that it is far better to endure trouble knowing that God is with me, than to try and handle life's most difficult moments without God. With God, there is always light in the midst of the darkness. Without

God, we are blinded by the trouble we see with our natural eyes and only see darkness and walk as blind fools.

---

*Without God, we are blinded by the trouble we see with our natural eyes and only see darkness and walk as blind fools.*

---

What's interesting about trouble is that it often ushers in our greatest moments of growth which makes a way for some of our greatest blessings. Most people do not instinctively think of pleasant thoughts when you talk about trouble. It is not the growth mechanism that we prefer. And perhaps our first line of response when trouble shows up is to pray that it goes away and to denounce the devil as the liar that he is. But before we take the road of declaring every troublesome situation as a demonic attack, could it be that there is something God intends to develop *in us* through the trouble? The Apostle Paul speaks of present sufferings as not worthy of comparison, to the glory that God will reveal *in us*. This means that the glorious work that God is doing in you will completely outweigh your present sufferings. That means that there is nothing happening in your life right now that God cannot use to shape your character and transform your heart. There is a greater outcome than what you can see. God's work in you is customized, based not only on your present but on your future in God that is yet to be revealed. God has a way of knowing what we need even when it doesn't match what we want. God knows what is necessary for our journey in spite of our preferences. God has a way of knowing just what is necessary for each of us to produce the character He desires, to produce the realization that our hope must be in nothing but God alone. God has a way of knitting together our trouble with our triumphs in such a way that you will know that only God could have orchestrated the events of your life. When this happens, there is a glory that is revealed in us that belongs only to the Lord. Like the psalmist King David declared, we will also conclude that "It was good for me to be afflicted" because affliction teaches humility and understanding of Godly character like nothing else can. (Psalm 119:71, NIV).

Trouble is necessary because it tests and increases our faith. Trouble is a filtration process, separating the grit from the water. Trouble clarifies what you need versus what can be discarded. Trouble allows God to purify our hearts. When things are at their worst that gives God an opportunity to show you His best. When it looks impossible, that gives God an opportunity to prove that with God all things are possible. As we grow our faith in God, we start seeing opportunities in the midst of great challenge. You will start seeing solutions in the midst of problems. You will see God illuminated in the midst of darkness, peace in the midst of chaos, and hope even in the midst of death.

On a cold Saturday morning in December of 2018, I was unsuccessful in reaching my mother on the phone. This was strange because it was our practice to talk daily, frequently multiple times a day. That morning I arrived at my mother's home where I unexpectedly found her deceased. In that moment, it seemed that the same house where it all started was the place where it all ended. You see, my mother's house was actually the same house that had been my Grandma Clary's house. The house became my mother's home when my Grandma Clary passed away years earlier. So now, I laid in the floor in a numbing shock just a few feet away from the kitchen table described in my introduction of this book, a place where I had gleaned so much perspective. Seven days later, I preached my mother's eulogy titled "The Most Precious Gifts" from 1 Corinthians 13:8–13, NIV. It is only because of God's strength that I was able to stand and declare His Word on this very difficult day. My mother's unexpected death was a test of my faith. She was the person that I called everyday as I drove home from work. Other than my sons, my mother was the only person who had truly witnessed an up close observance of my transformation in God. She saw my previous foolish ways and then she had the privilege to see me come into an understanding of the woman I am in God. There are some things that only a mother is able to understand and she knew me better than any other human being on earth. I had ministered to many who had experienced the loss of a loved one, encouraging them to be comforted by God's love. Now, I was in need of comfort and had to exercise the faith that I had preached to others about. I give God glory, honor, and praise because God proved himself faithful and allowed me to stand in a strength that I can only describe as supernatural. There is not a word that I can articulate to describe what I experienced. God delivered a message through me that not only encouraged others, but allowed me to step into a newer deeper experience with Him. There are some levels of faith that are only attained through a process of testing and fire. This type of faith is not produced from times of ease and comfort. The trouble is necessary.

Trouble is also necessary because it teaches us that we must be careful how we handle frustrations. We can't always control what happens to us, but we can control how we respond when trouble arises. For the believer, trouble teaches us that there is no frustration in this world that should speak louder to us than the God who established our hope and our future. It is in moments of frustration that our flesh and our spirit collide the greatest. The areas within us that have been disciplined spiritually are in direct opposition to our foolish tendencies of the flesh that still remain. "For what the flesh desires is opposed to the Spirit, and what the Spirit desires is opposed to the flesh; for these are opposed to each other to prevent you from doing what you want" (Galatians 5:17, NRSV). When we face this war within, we must decide to be led by the Spirit. The frustration that we experience during trouble is to push us towards God, and the future we have in Him. The frustration that you feel in times of trouble is not to push you towards foolish behaviors or cause you to be immobilized and fearful to walk forward. Don't let the frustration of your present, rob you of the glory that God wants to reveal in your future. When you experience seasons of trouble, you must decide if you are going to draw closer to God or go in the opposite direction trying to rely on your own strength. To do the latter, you become a pawn in the enemy's scheme against you to rob you of your peace, rob you of your joy, and rob you of your faith and your belief in the truth of God's Word and God's power. Times of trouble are no time to give up. If you've been foolish, it's no time to beat yourself up. It's time to seek God like you have never sought Him before!

Lastly, trouble is necessary because it precipitates great change and creates opportunities for the miraculous. There are some changes that you have not been prompted to make until trouble showed up. For some, had it not been for the trouble, you would not have surrendered your life to God. It was only after trying to handle the troubles of life without God, did you realize that you needed God. Some of the greatest shifts towards positive change that we have seen over the course of history have been on the heels of great trouble. The context of numerous biblical accounts is inclusive of the backdrop of troublesome times. However, trouble is not a guarantee that change will occur. Trouble sets the atmosphere for the opportunity of change to take place. However, it is possible to experience great trouble as a result of sin and refuse to change, falling into a debased mindset (Romans 1:28, NKJV). This is when you have come into the knowledge of God but have decided to reject God and His ways for your life. People who have fallen into a debased mind do not feel any conviction from the Holy Spirit because their rejection of God and sin has caused a separation from truth. Not only do things look right in their own eyes, but there is also a replacement of right with wrong giving wrong the label of right.

While I do not believe that it is the nature of God to send trouble for harm, God will allow trouble to exist to bring about change in us that is honorable to God. But oddly enough, along with trouble comes the opportunity for a miracle. One of my favorite biblical stories is that of Hannah which is found in the Old Testament book of 1 Samuel. Hannah's name literally means favor or grace in the Hebrew.[22] But interestingly, Hannah's story reveals to us that her favor is disguised in a miserable messed-up situation. This story unfolds in a time of instability and uncertainty, prior to the first king of Israel and described in the last verse of the book of Judges as a time where "everyone did what was right in his own eyes (Judges 21:25, NKJV)." According to Proverbs 12:15 (NKJV), it is the way of a fool that looks right in one's own eyes, and those who heed to Godly counsel who is wise. The story of Hannah is a story of a woman who experienced barrenness, breaking, and yet outrageous blessings during a time where wisdom was scarce and foolishness was plentiful. At first glance, it would seem that the first two experiences of barrenness and breaking do not belong with the later experience of outrageous blessings. But let us take a closer look at how God will blow our mind when

---

[22] Matthew George Easton, The New Easton's Bible Dictionary (Ontario, Canada: Electronic Christian Media, 2016).

we continually seek God with unabashed prayer in the midst of great distress.

Not only did Hannah carry the mark of being barren in a society that placed a woman's value on her ability to have children, Hannah's husband Elkanah took a second wife named Penninah who was very fruitful, bearing multiple children. As if things couldn't get any worse, Penninah took great pleasure in constantly taunting Hannah because of her barrenness. Hannah's barrenness not only represents her inability to have a child, it is a representation of the promise she believed God for but just couldn't seem to grasp all while enduring daily persecution in some very difficult circumstances. If you've ever had to endure some troublesome circumstances and felt like you just couldn't seem to get the blessing while those around you were being blessed with what you desired, then you may be able to relate to Hannah's dilemma. One might ask, why does it seem that at times the one who strives to live by Godly principles has to endure so much and can't seem to receive the blessing and those that are intent on persecuting you seem to be dripping in the very blessings you desire? My brothers and sisters, God says that what you see is only a splinter of what you think you see. We see in part, God sees in total. We examine the physical, but God reveals in the spiritual. Our understanding is incomplete, yet God's complete plans for our life is far greater than what our minds are even capable of imaging.

I love this story because it shows us how God's grace and

favor will sustain us even while dealing with trouble. The double portion of provisions that Hannah received reveals God's hand in the midst of her trouble. This double portion was sustaining for a while but at some point, Hannah reaches a breaking point and her desperation leads her to the feet of God. Whether we realize it or not, we all have breaking points, thresholds of breaking that require a strength greater than ourselves. Hannah prays with such anguish and grief that the priest who was watching thought that she was drunk because her mouth was moving but no words were coming out. There is a level of trouble and pain so great that even at the feet of God, you have no articulation of speech and it is the Holy Spirit that searches your heart and intercedes on your behalf. This level of pain is not concerned with what other people think or having elaborate words. This was Hannah's breaking point and God used her breaking to orchestrate a miraculous breakthrough. Only God can use your breaking point, the moment when you feel that you are at the end of your rope, and turn it into a breakthrough for a miraculous new beginning. Not only did Hannah miraculously bear a son from a womb that had been closed, God outrageously blessed Hannah with not just any son but a son who would become the prophet Samuel who would anoint David as King as part of God's strategic lineage of Jesus. The miracle was only made possible by the trouble. The difficulty is that we must trust the providence of God even when we see no indication of the promise, no evidence of the change, and when the womb is still empty.

Despite the magnification of any present trouble, if we pause just for a moment we may recall God's track record of faithfulness throughout the Bible and what God has already done in our own lives. We may recall that God has brought many of us from a mighty long way, called us out of some places where only God's arms could stretch to reach us. We may discover that there have been more wins than losses, more good than bad, and more grace than we can account for. So, we can't allow trouble to cheapen our faith when God's grace and mercy continue to remain with us. "Surely, goodness and mercy shall follow me all the days of my life (Psalm 23:6, NKJV)" Gods goodness is not dependent on your circumstances and God's mercy is not dependent on if your situation changes. Gods goodness and mercy are with you right now for all of the days of your life, not just some, but all.

The strategy of God is greater than the pain of your trouble. You have no idea of the level of blessing that God will release to you through your trouble. Don't allow the magnitude of the trouble to cause you to quit too soon and forfeit the miracle. Instead seek God with a desperation and commitment to glorify God with every blessing received, while you are waiting on the blessing you've prayed for to arrive. I challenge you to be more desperate for God, than for the blessings of God. When we have God, we have access to everything that God has for our lives. Before we become overwhelmed with the latest breaking news, God is reminding us to remember his track record of faithfulness. Before we allow any present circumstance to cause us to quit on life, God is saying I have not brought you this far to leave you. In fact, I the Lord God Almighty, have called you as my sons and daughters for such a time as this.

**Questions for your consideration …**

1. How can you use the trouble in your life to reveal the glory of God in you?

2. How has trouble shaped your character? In what ways has trouble pushed you closer to God?

3. What step is God inviting you to take next?

#  Prayer & Praise

Father God, your Word says "Whoever dwells in the shelter of the Most High will rest in the shadow of the Almighty. I will say of the Lord, He is my refuge and my fortress, my God in whom I trust (Psalms 91:1–2, NIV)." I am desperate for your presence Lord. Help me to fix my eyes not on what is seen, but on what is unseen, since what is seen is temporary, and it is the eternal that is unseen. Lord help me to recognize the permanent from that which is temporary. Thank you God that no trouble lasts always and that every trouble has an expiration date. I set my eyes on the peace of God, that surpasses understanding and on the Word of God that is a lamp to my feet and a light to my path. Help me Lord to allow the process to shape my character and prune what's not needed for my future. I praise you God in advance for the glory that will be revealed in me. I count it all joy. In the name of Jesus. Amen.

# Chapter 7

# Challenging Your Status Quo and Living as an Heir

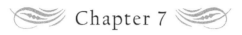

Throughout the book, I have challenged you to see yourself beyond every mistake you've made in life and beyond those that you may make in your future. I've tried to invite you to see yourself as God sees you. As Paul wrote nearly two thousand years ago, most of us can acknowledge that at one time or another we too were once foolish, disobedient, deceived and enslaved by all kinds of passions and pleasures. Without God we walk as blind fools.

As an heir in God, we have access to wisdom and spiritual weapons that help us to walk in the promises of God. We are beneficiaries of the new covenant through Jesus made available by His death on the cross for the whosoever that believes and through His resurrection. There are spiritual benefits available to those who are joint heirs with Christ Jesus. Through the gift of the Holy Spirit, we have power, protection, and peace. We have access to a power that is greater than ourselves, to a sovereign protection in God's promise to be with us, and to a peace that defies human understanding because of our hope and faith in God. As a believer, we are more than conquerors, which means that with God we can not only overcome but we can live life in the "more than" and in the "more abundantly" that Jesus came to give (Romans 8:37, NIV). This remains true even during unprecedented times of adversity and through great challenge.

---

*It is always the right time and the right season to walk in the will of God for your life.*

---

As an heir, we also have a responsibility to live our best life yet. This means that we can no longer settle for the status quo of just enough, when we are purposed and being called to something greater. It is always the right time and the right season to walk in the will of God for your life. In God's will, we are able to authentically develop and strive towards the best version of ourselves, revealed through the Holy Spirit and mirroring the likeness of Christ. The Apostle Paul speaks of our inheritance in Ephesians Chapter 5. We as dearly loved children of God are to follow God's example and walk in love. The responsibility of being an heir necessitates that we allow the wisdom of God to guide our lives and make the most of every opportunity. Therefore, do not be foolish, but

understand what the Lord's will is (Ephesians 5:17, NIV)."
In the Lord's will, you will find hope and assurance that God
is with you and faithful to His Word, that is unable to return
void.

These are a few strategies that I believe will help you embark
on your best life yet.

**Begin your day with prayer.**

> Allow your first words spoken to be offering of
> thanksgiving to God for His love. Begin your day
> thanking God for the opportunity of another new
> day to live a life that honors God. Commit to a daily
> designated time of devotion. Just remember that God
> is present and available outside of your scheduled time!

**Develop the discipline of reading and studying the Word
of God.**

> Do not place your total reliance on the pastor's preached
> interpretation of the Word. Know and understand the
> Word of God for yourself. As an heir, you have bold
> access to our Father God. The veil has been torn and
> we are able to enter the Holy of Holies. As you engage
> in the intimate presence of God and with the Word of
> God, you will experience the revelation of God anew!

## Walk in bold confidence as God's very own.

This is not walking in arrogance and pride. This is having a bold confidence in who God says you are and not allowing yourself to be defined by the world's standards. You are much more than people's opinions and the number of social media likes! Your validation comes from God!

## Seek God's Will.

The safest place to exist on earth is when our will is aligned with God's will. We are most powerful when we walk authentically in the will of God. The Holy Spirit intercedes on our behalf in accordance with the will of God. Not our will, God's will.

## Examine Your Circle.

It's time to move on from people who are only able to see you through the limited lens of how they've once known you. Surround yourself with people who have beat the odds and can support your God given potential. Connect with those who will sincerely seek God on your behalf without the interference of their familiarity with your previous self or their personal insecurities or agenda.

**Complete the Process.**

When trouble comes, face it knowing that God is with you. Place your hope in God and allow the process to accomplish something great in you. Allow the testing of your faith to draw you closer to God and to strengthen your convictions. If you short circuit the process, you may also hinder your growth and clip your potential.

**Reach high!**

There is nothing about God that is mediocre! As an Heir, you are called to stretch forward towards your full God given potential. Don't settle for the status quo of easy and comfortable when God is calling you to greater! Stretch toward the mark that God has set before you.

Your obedience will be required. Might I remind you that our processes of spiritual transformation are not isolated to an event, but occur in an imperfect step by step manner with an intentional focus on God. When you get it right, praise God and celebrate what God is doing in your life. When you get it wrong, seek forgiveness and praise God for another opportunity to get it right. But never stop seeking to walk in the will of God. Whatever you do, never ever give up and quit, because God will not give up and quit on you.

Be aware, that everyone will not celebrate your growth. You may be surprised by who will become envious or insecure because of your growth. Some people's vision will be stuck at the station in life where they experienced life with you. Some will be uncomfortable with your growth in God because it will cause them to examine their relationship and walk with God. Some people will be your supporters as long as God does not elevate you beyond what they believe you deserve. Don't allow the insecurities of others to stunt what God desires to do through your life. Walk in your redemption and humbly receive your restoration. All while understanding that the blessings God bestows to you are never just about you. It is for those who are watching and may see the power of God in your life and be drawn to God themselves. When we choose life and blessings, God will extend the benefits of your choice to your descendants and those you are connected to (Deuteronomy 30:19, NKJV). We do not exist in this world alone but in strategic connection with other human beings. Living as an heir comes with the responsibility to authentically be who God has called you to be, so that others may see, and come into the marvelous light of God. I implore you to speak life and be light to those whom you encounter. Whatever it is that you are supposed to be doing with your life, get to it! I do not know what your "it" is but the breath in your body is evidence that you still have an "it". You can't wait for them to fix it or change. Trust me, it's not about them. It's about what God wants to do in and through you. Time is a precious gift extended to us from our creator

God who is not bound by the parameters of time. So, do not waste it on the superficial, inconsequential, or the ineffectual. If today were your last, how would you honor God with your life? Live today with the passion and urgency that comes with the realization of your brevity of life on earth, and with the security of God's promise of your eternal life through salvation in the name of Jesus Christ.

My challenge to you is to take the step God has been calling you to take, knowing that God is with you and able to catch you. My prayer for you is that after having read this book, your "Now What" will be to go and live your best life yet. I pray that you will go after that dream that you have been sitting on. You will take a step of obedience into your future, despite every obstacle or injury you have faced and those that you will face. I pray that you will walk in the blessed assurance of knowing that God is with you and that as God's very own possession, you are created on purpose and called for a purpose in God. I pray that you will seek God in a new way and align your will with that of the Father. "Forsake foolishness and live, and go in the way of true understanding" (Proverbs 9:6, NKJV). Stay focused and attuned to God's voice and you will win!

**Questions for your consideration ...**

1. How have you been challenged to move beyond the status quo, mediocre, and just enough in your life towards greater?

2. What are some changes that will help you to develop and reach your full potential in God? What immediate steps will you take towards change?

3. How can you use what God is doing in your life to speak life to others?

# Prayer & Praise

To the one and only true and living God, I thank you for every word that speaks life and your truth that you have allowed me to read. God, I thank you for every revelation and insight. I'm grateful that I still have an opportunity to live my best life yet. I can still make the adjustment. I can still turn towards Jesus the High Priest and glorify God with my life. Now Father God, let your glory fill me and be revealed in me. Let your transforming power be evident in me and through me. Lord bless those who will see your transformation in me with the opportunity to turn towards Jesus and worship You God. To God be the glory for all the things You have done, and all that You have spoken. In the name of Jesus. Amen.

# Epilogue

This book was completed during the midst of the Covid-19 global pandemic and great social unrest throughout the Nation, spurred by the persistent issue of race in America. As people deal with a myriad of feelings and circumstances surrounding these galvanizing issues, we can place our hope in the unchangeable truth that God is in control. The ministry of Jesus was closely connected to those who experienced sickness and death, as well as those who were marginalized and devalued by society. Although I've carried this book in my belly for years, by no means is it an accident that I've been able to give birth to this book during such a tumultuous time in history. Many who have disregarded God are rethinking and reconsidering their views on spirituality and church. Some who have previously rejected Jesus are seeking to know Him in the power of His resurrection. People are being humbled by the magnificence of God and the limitations of self. Those who have knowledge of God and who had walked away from their foundation of faith, are finding it necessary to return to God and that they would rather have the peace of God than silver, gold, or any possession. The "fierce urgency of now" that Dr. Martin Luther King spoke about during his 1963 March on

Washington speech still remains relevant and is seen through a renewed search for hope, healing, and change.[23] Jesus and the love of God was the answer over two thousand years ago and remains the answer for today.

"For the message of the cross is foolishness to those who are perishing, but to us who are being saved it is the power of God" (1 Corinthians 1:18, NIV). The idea that Jesus and the love of God are the answer to the complexities of our current reality is contrary to the wisdom that the world teachers. However, the wisdom of God is never out of style and will always frustrate intellectualism. Yet, the commonality of human kind is that we are drawn to something that is greater than ourselves. It is the immeasurable love of God that fulfills this need, and it is the love of God that continues to overcome the world and its troublesome circumstances. God's love cannot be neatly placed in a box based on our human parameters but it is a love that extends beyond barriers of race, denomination, and gender. If our religion, beliefs, and foundation do not demonstrate the love of God and unity across barriers, it is not reflective of Jesus Christ and dishonors God. Perhaps the greatest "Now What" that we must all embrace is to love God with all of our heart, mind, and soul and then to love others as ourselves. If we truly do this, we have learned to value what God values and we would have done our part to fulfill the great command of God with our lives. God is our certainty in times of uncertainty, stability

---

[23] King, Martin L., Jr. "I Have a Dream." Speech. Lincoln Memorial, Washington, D. C. 28 Aug. 1963.

in times of instability. God is our surety and our hope. As you move forward, "May the Lord bless you and keep you, the Lord make His face to shine upon you and be gracious to you; the Lord lift up His countenance upon you, and give you peace" (Numbers 6:24–26, NKJV). Amen.

# Notes

## Introduction

1   Howard Thurman, Jesus and the Disinherited, (Boston, Massachusetts: Beacon Press, 1996).

2   Etymology Online Dictionary, https://www.etymonline.com/search?q=fool

3   https://www.biblica.com/resources/scholar-notes/niv-study-bible/intro-to-titus/

4   Based on the King James Version of the Bible

5   Pablo Freire, Pedagogy of the Oppressed (New York: Continuum, 2000).

## Chapter 1 - The Power of Understanding Your Identity in God.

1   What is you Life's Blueprint?, Seattle Times, https://projects.seattletimes.com/mlk/words-blueprint.html

## Chapter 2 - Religion *Alone* Is Not Enough

1   Christopher Patridge, Introduction to World Religions (Minneapolis, MN: Fortress Press, 2018).

2   W. F. Conton, West Africa in History, Vol. I, Before 1800, (Allen & Unwin Academic, 2019).

3    Richard Brown, The Door of No Return, Commonweal Magazine, May 8, 2017. Retrieved 7/28/2020, commonwealmagazine.org/door-no-return

4    1 Corinthians 12:12 – 31 compares the human body and all its many parts to the church, which is referred to the body of Christ.

## Chapter 3 - It's Not Just You

1    199 references are found in the King James Version of the Bible.

2    Butterfly Story retrieved from http://instructor.mstc.edu/instructor/swallerm/Struggle%20-%20Butterfly.htm#:~:text=Every%20day%20he%20watched%20the,it%20new%20plants%20to%20eat.&text=The%20boy%20worriedly%20called%20his,metamorphosis%20and%20become%20a%20butterfly.

## Chapter 4 - Replacing Old Thoughts

1    Parable of the Sower and the Seed, Luke 8:4 –15

## Chapter 5 - Perfection Is Not the Requirement - So What Is?

1    Strong's Exhaustive Concordance: New American Standard Bible. 1995. Updated ed. L Habra: Lockman Foundation. http://www.biblestudytools.com/concordances/strongs-exhaustive-concordance/.

2    https://www.preceptaustin.org/love-agape

3    Diane Wolkstein, Step by Step (New York: Morrow Junior Books, 1994).

## Chapter 6 - The Truth about Trouble: It Is Necessary

1   Matthew George Easton, The New Easton's Bible Dictionary (Ontario, Canada: Electronic Christian Media, 2016).

## Epilogue

1   King, Martin L., Jr. "I Have a Dream." Speech. Lincoln Memorial, Washington, D. C. 28 Aug. 1963.